Love

Coloring Book

Love

Coloring Book

SIRIUS

SIRIUS

This edition published in 2022 by Sirius Publishing, a division of
Arcturus Publishing Limited,
26/27 Bickels Yard, 151–153 Bermondsey Street,
London SE1 3HA

Copyright © Arcturus Holdings Limited

ISBN: 978-1-3988-2246-7
CH007281NT
Supplier 29, Date 0622, PI00002224

Printed in China

Introduction

You'll find that love is all around when you open this coloring book packed with images of hearts, flowers, romantic abstracts, and dreamy mandalas. Let your emotions take center stage as you focus on adding color to the gorgeous patterns and discover a tranquil, feel-good state of mind.

Like a surprise bunch of flowers or a lighthouse in a stormy sea, these pages offer a happy refuge from an often demanding and stress-filled world.

So take the plunge and discover your inner softie. All you need is love (and a set of colored pens or pencils).

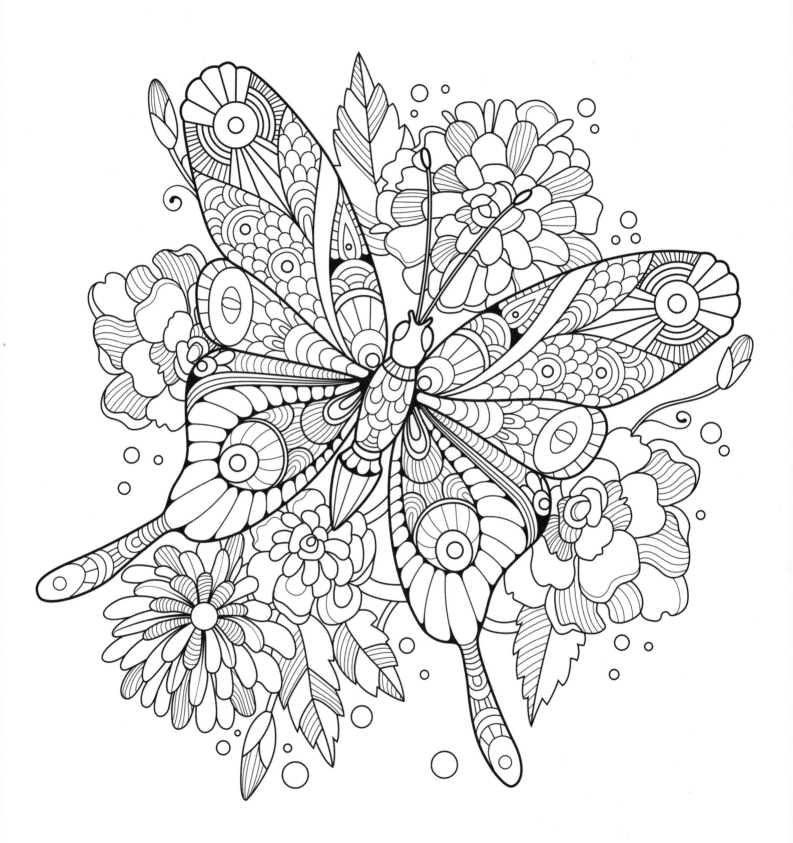

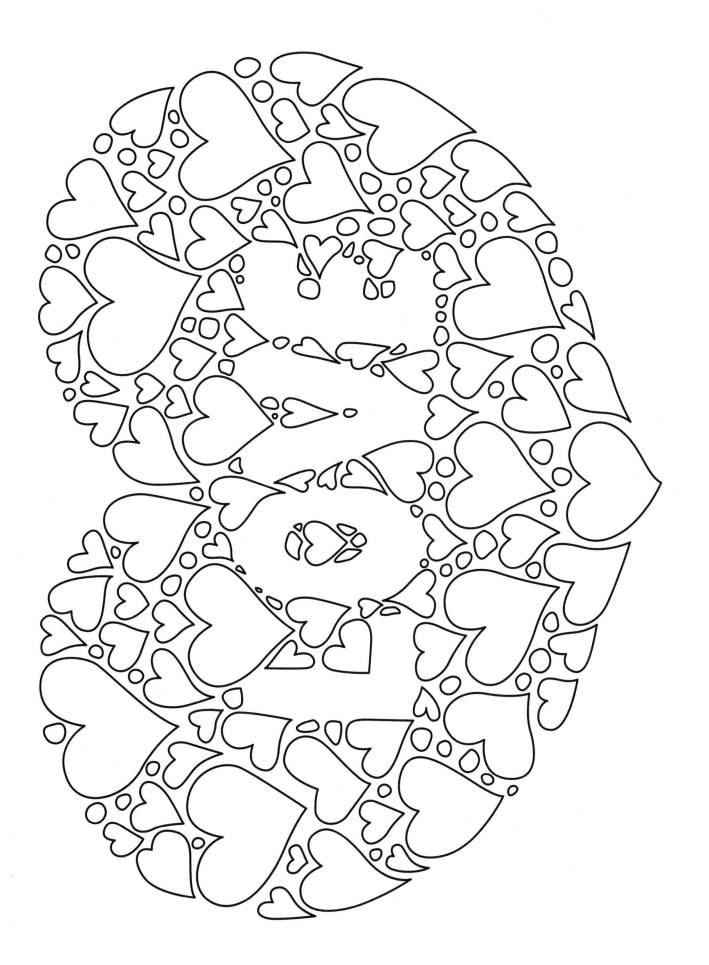